GIFTS from the Heart

A Collection of Stories that Touch the Heart

Gathered by

• *Melly Kinnard* •

KENDALL/HUNT PUBLISHING COMPANY
4050 Westmark Drive   Dubuque, Iowa 52002

Copyright © 1998 by Marie L. (Melly) Kinnard

Library of Congress Catalog Card Number: 97-74896

ISBN 0-7872-4423-6

All rights reserved. No part of this publication may be reproduced, stored in a retrieval system, or transmitted, in any form or by any means, electronic, mechanical, photocopying, recording, or otherwise, without the prior written permission of the copyright owner.

Printed in the United States of America
10 9 8 7 6 5 4 3 2 1

A gift from the heart is given with no thought

of receiving anything in return.

Dan McGreevy and His Goddaughter

My brother, Dan McGreevy, is an attorney in Bellingham, Washington. In the fall of 1985, after the seafood business in Alaska slowed down, Dan decided to take the winter off to travel. He started in Seattle, explored San Francisco, continued to Montreal, where our mother was born and raised, then on to London and Florence, where he had been a student in 1970–1971. February 13, 1986, Dan was in Le Havre, France, boarding a ship for Rosslare, Ireland when he met "Sean" and "Karen." Karen was eight months pregnant.

Dan spent the night in Rosslare. Since the train for Dublin didn't depart until three in the afternoon, he had a good part of the day to explore. Everyone he passed on the street greeted him. People passing in their cars nodded or waved. Dan immediately felt at home in the country of his ancestors.

Arriving back at the train station, Dan found Sean and Karen, who were planning on taking the same train to Dublin. They continued talking on the train. Dan learned that both were American students. When

Karen became pregnant she and Sean didn't want to tell their parents about the pregnancy. They told their parents they wanted to take a quarter off from college and travel in Europe. Neither set of parents was pleased. When Karen's pregnancy began to be obvious, the young couple left for Europe.

Sean was born in Ireland and had a grandmother in Dublin. He had an Irish passport. In Ireland the cost of hospitalization for an unwed mother was free to the mother since the cost was absorbed by the Irish government. They had planned for Karen to have the baby in Ireland and give the baby up for adoption there. They confided in Dan that they had recently been to Ireland to see Sean's grandmother and were concerned about the poverty. They were afraid to leave their baby in a country where they felt it might not have many advantages. They hadn't started the adoption process and would have preferred to have the baby adopted by Americans but didn't know how to proceed.

Dan told them about his friends in Oregon who had a ten year old son and had been unsuccessful in adopting a child. Dan asked if they would like him to call "Tom" and "Ann" to see if they would like to adopt the baby. The prospective parents enthusiastically agreed. Tom and Ann were thrilled with the possibility of becoming adoptive parents. They asked Dan to give them more information about the health and family histories of Sean and Karen.

Dan had planned to spend a few months in Ireland, possibly starting a doctoral program. Until he found an apartment to rent, he, Sean and Karen stayed in the same hotel. Karen planned to stay in a convent for the final weeks until the baby was born. Sean planned to stay with his grandmother during that time. Dan's new landlord was an Irish solicitor, who agreed to handle the legal details. Dan, Sean and Karen met almost daily to tour Dublin, share meals and sample stout. Dan quickly felt at home in Ireland among the fair skin, red hair and ruddy cheeks. He ventured to Northern Ireland to try to better understand the conflict with the English.

On February 27, 1986, Dan had planned to travel to Dun Boyne to visit Karen in the convent. Before he was fully awake, Dan was awakened by his landlord who shouted, "The child has been born! It is extremely urgent that you ring Sean back!" Dan threw on his clothes and tried to call Sean at his grandmother's home. She didn't know where Sean was. Assuming the baby was born in Dun Boyne, Dan took the bus to rural Dun Boyne. At the convent Dan learned that Karen had been transferred to a hospital in Dublin. Dan returned to his apartment to await Sean's call. Dan rushed to Coombe hospital and was able to hold the infant girl who had arrived prematurely and hadn't opened her eyes yet. Fortunately the legal adoption paperwork had arrived the day of the birth. After numerous attempts, Dan was able to get through to Tom and Ann to tell them of their daughter's birth. They booked an immediate flight to Dublin after Dan had talked at length with the new parents who agreed they still would give the baby up for adoption.

The reunion at the Dublin airport with Dan, Tom and Ann was joyous. The three had dinner and made plans to meet the next day when Karen and the infant were released from the hospital. During the discharge procedure, an administrator from the hospital congratulated all involved on having everything correctly handled according to Irish and U.S. law. Karen handed her infant daughter to Dan, who placed the precious life in the arms of her new mother. The following day Tom and Ann met at the U.S. Embassy to have documents signed, notarized and to obtain a U.S. passport for the newborn. Joy and sadness consumed Dan as he parted from the couple when they flew home to the U.S. with their miracle baby.

March 11, 1986 was the last time Dan saw Sean and Karen. Dan felt the void of loneliness as he said good–bye to two friends with whom he had shared a profound experience.

Dan is the godfather of this well–loved child and continues to be involved in her life.

A child fills a special place inside your heart

A place you never knew was empty.

By Michael O'Neill
(Catholic priest from Kalispell, Montana)

In late November of 1982, I had the terrible misfortune of contracting the life threatening disease of hepatitis. Within three months my liver was destroyed and I was given three weeks to live. My only hope for survival was to have a liver transplant, which was relatively unknown in Montana. My choices were death, or the high risk of an experimental transplantation. After much prayer and a lot of support from family and friends, I made the decision to go to Pittsburgh and have the liver transplant. In March of 1983, I had a successful liver transplant after fourteen hours of surgery and three and a half months in the hospital. This was the most challenging, difficult and toughest experience of my life. I received my greatest and most meaningful gift, the gift of my new liver. To me this had been the "gift of life."

In order for me to live, someone else had to die – a sobering and disturbing thought. To be a donor is to make a commitment of total giving of self. This needs to be thought out well before death is near. The donor needs to make these wishes known to family members. In my case, the donor's family told me they were able to make more sense out of their family member's death knowing that my life was continuing due to the transplant. What a tremendous gift! Out of death comes life.

Later I named my new liver "John," which means "gift from God." Through prayer I introduced "John" to the rest of my body. I have a quality of life that I thought I would never experience again. This experience has changed my life. I know and appreciate life in a much fuller way. I see and experience life as a precious gift. Life is fragile and for that reason each day is a tremendous gift. This gift of "John" is truly a gift from the heart.

May soft be the grass you walk on

May fair be the skies above you

May true be the joys that surround you

May dear be the hearts that love you.

Irish Blessing

Gary VanderArk, M.D.

Gary VanderArk moved to Denver after neurosurgical training in Ann Arbor, Michigan and Walter Reed Hospital in Washington, D.C. At 33, his first job was at Denver General Hospital which served the poor of Denver. Gary loved his time at Denver General due to the esprit de corps among the staff. He was proud of the excellent care given to patients without consideration of their ability to pay.

Gary's goal was to climb the academic ladder of neurosurgery. In 1976, he was offered chairmanships outside of Denver. His wife and two high school children didn't want to leave Denver. So Gary went into private practice and learned the complexity of having employees, paying the high cost of malpractice insurance and other intricacies of running a practice. While he had been in the Army Medical Corps, no patient had been asked if he had insurance before they received care. Gary was bothered by the financial aspects of private patient care. He missed dealing with patients without consideration of financial resources.

Gary's vision was to provide health care for the working poor, those who fell through the cracks in the system. He began serving on committees for the medically indigent through the Colorado Hospital Association, Colorado Medical Society and Denver Medical Society. For thirty years Denver has been a model for providing care for the medically indigent. In the late sixties Public Health Service gave grants to provide care for the poor. Denver was the first city to develop neighborhood health centers. Gary wanted to reach out to the suburbs where large pockets of poverty existed. In 1986, Public Health approved funding for the first clinic in Aurora, a Denver suburb. Gary fought for duplicate service in Jefferson and Arapahoe counties.

In 1987, Denver General Hospital and University Hospital got in an argument when University Hospital announced they would no longer treat Denver's poor. Denver General responded in outrage and said they would no longer treat patients who lived outside the city of Denver's boundaries. Christmas of 1987 found people living in Denver's suburbs unable to go to a hospital or neighborhood health center. This was a crisis situation.

Gary met with the administrators of Porter and Swedish Hospitals (in Arapahoe County). Since Gary was the president of the Arapahoe Medical Society at the time, he had a favorable position for negotiating. He was stunned when Porter and Swedish gave him full support. They offered to cover laboratory tests, x-rays and hospitalization to indigent patients referred to them.

In January of 1988, Gary invited 350 physicians in Arapahoe County to help. He asked each doctor to do their part so no one would be overburdened. He asked the doctors to call him if they did not want to be part of this program. He said if he didn't hear from them he assumed they agreed to be part of the program. From the first day he had a large pool of doctors willing to see indigent patients.

If patients needed health care, they went to the Arapahoe Medical Society for intake interviews conducted by volunteers, who were doctors' wives. Jayne Howard, Associate Director of the Arapahoe Medical Society, named this new project Doctors Care, which began February 14, 1988.

Every patient was assigned a primary care physician. Every specialty was represented as part of this program. No public announcement was made for fear of being overwhelmed by patients. Gary told Interfaith Task Force, Tri County Health Department and school nurses. Doctors Care was ready to see patients.

An unforeseen problem arose. After being seen by

the physicians, the patients needed prescriptions they couldn't afford. Gary went back to Swedish Hospital and was given $25,000 from the Swedish Foundation to cover the cost of prescriptions for that first year. Nick Hilger, past Swedish administrator, was Gary's ally from the beginning. When Littleton Hospital (part of the Porter system) opened in 1991, they came on board. Gary's goal was to have 500 patients in the program at the end of the first year. There were 700. At the end of the second year there were 1,200.

The first few years the program was run by a committee of Arapahoe Medical Society members. They formed a community board with representation from Interfaith Task Force, Tri County Health, the Junior League of Denver, the League of Women Voters and the Colorado Legislature.

Doctors Care has become a true community project involving many volunteer organizations. Gary went to every Lions, Sertoma and Rotary organization who invited him to speak. In 1989 the Junior League of Denver took on Doctors Care as a project. Sixty League volunteers offered time, talent and $10,000 a year. When the League takes on a project, it agrees to fund it financially and with volunteers for three years. At the end of their three years so many volunteers wanted to continue that the League made an exception and agreed to spend six years with Doctors Care. The League came in and found a simple operation with everything in a black book. They told Gary his project needed to be run like a business and a computer was needed. The League purchased the software and then input all the records into the computer. Gary feels his association with the League is a "marriage made in heaven." During the spring of 1996 the League turned over the operation to Littleton Sertoma volunteers. Gary said he would give the League a three-year respite, then wanted them back.

In 1992, it became apparent that the pediatricians were overburdened. Pediatricians are the least able to take on the poor since they are often overwhelmed with operating their busy practices. Gary went back to Swedish Hospital and asked for donated space in a building Swedish leases at 191 East Orchard Road in Arapahoe County. He opened a sick child clinic in the space. It is on a bus line and is located at a convenient site for the people served. Swedish also pays for the phone service and utilities. Two child health care associates staff the clinic with a receptionist who views her position as her mission rather than a job.

Almost three million dollars in free medical care is provided by Doctors Care on an annual basis. The working sick who fall through the cracks, those without the safety net of Medicaid or welfare benefits are helped. The majority of patients are young working families who don't have medical insurance.

There is not a community in Colorado that doesn't have a program for the medically indigent. In

Boulder, Colorado, Physicians Care is based on the Denver project. There are 450 doctors and three hospitals taking part in this program.

The hardest part, Gary has found, is keeping the doctors involved. The poor don't keep appointments and aren't as compliant about following the doctors' instructions for taking medications and related suggestions. The receptionist at Doctors Care calls to remind patients to come to appointments and take their medications. The patients pay $2.00 for each prescription and $5.00 for each office visit if they are able. During the initial interview the patients are asked to pay on a sliding scale. Some patients pay 50% and some pay 25%, but most pay nothing.

Doctors Care takes pride in operating a huge program on a small budget. Most physicians go into medicine for altruistic reasons. In addition to donating time, these physicians donate money personally and through the Arapahoe Medical Society.

Gary VanderArk is a man who saw a need and asked for what he needed.

IT was in my heart to help a little

because I was helped much.

Kahlil Gibran

Bryn Sara Linkow

During Bryn Linkow's junior year as an English major at Vanderbilt University she was forced to return home due to her lengthy battle with ulcerative colitis. Susie, Bryn's mother, saw the pain in Bryn's face as the drugs flowed through a permanent tube in her chest. Bryn didn't complain. Susie and Mark, Bryn's father, and Matt, her younger brother, tried to be with her continuously to ease her discomfort. Susie had nightmares about Bryn dying. A month before her twentieth birthday, Bryn ended her life after being worn down by this illness. She had a rare window of opportunity when she was alone for a brief time. Matt discovered his best friend and sister's still body. The day before her death Bryn sent her parents and Matt flowers. Looking back, Susie realized Bryn had contacted many friends to say good–bye.

Bryn's stunning beauty was apparent. Her spiritual

beauty was treasured by those fortunate to be touched by her life. Academically and artistically brilliant, her exceptional art work is proudly displayed in her parents' home. The Rhode Island School of Design was one of the competitive schools where she was accepted. She chose Vanderbilt, which she entered with sophomore standing due to her high school achievements.

Bryn's friends cherished their close friendships. Pablo Neruda was her favorite poet, "Forever Young" her favorite song. Late one night Bryn burst into her home cradling a near–dead rabbit she had found after it had been struck by a car. She pleaded with her parents to help her save this helpless animal she had rescued from an asphalt grave.

When Susie, Mark and Matt learned of Bryn's death, they immediately called their closest friends, Janie Butterly and Steven and Robin Chotin, who rushed over to offer help. The Chotins quickly turned this unfathomable tragedy into something positive by establishing the Bryn Sara Linkow Foundation. They knew how upset Bryn was by the plight of dedicated students unable to return to Vanderbilt due to financial hardship. The Chotin Group absorbs the administrative costs so that 100% of all donations fund scholarships of $5,000, to be used for one or two scholarships. Vanderbilt University, Washington University in St. Louis, where Matt Linkow is now a student, and Syracuse University, where the Chotins' oldest daughter, Mauri, is a student, charge no fee to administer the scholarships. Since so many Denver residents fund the scholarships, the Linkows have also started funding scholarships at the University of Denver.

The Linkows have met many of the scholars and have received touching letters. The students share their aspirations, college activities and appreciation for easing the financial burden at these costly private universities. One student, Dara Hammond, of Vanderbilt, wrote "I owe a thank you to Bryn for her compassion and recognition of the financial plight of many Vanderbilt students. Because of your kindness, her soul is very much alive and will now help me toward a better future. The photograph of your family is the only photograph I have on my mirror. Your family is the first people I see every morning, and it serves as a daily reminder to me that I would conceivably not be here without your help. I hope in some small way I will make you glad and proud that you chose to support my efforts here."

The Director of Donor Relations at Vanderbilt said, "Since Bryn was an outstanding scholar, it is fitting that a scholarship named for her will assist students who love learning and excel academically."

A Syracuse University official pledged: "This money will keep deserving students where they belong – in school."

Creating the foundation has been therapeutic for the

Linkow family. Susie took a short leave from her career as a bookkeeper at the Chotin Group. She would force herself to get dressed and keep appointments with bankers who didn't know how raw her emotions were. For months she could barely focus. Reading was not possible but she was able to do math calculations. Returning to the Chotin Group in such a supportive environment, helped Susie keep her sanity. "Creating the scholarships has been a wonderful experience for us," Susie said. "It has made some sense out of our tragedy. It enables us to do something for these kids who are amazing in so many ways." Mark added, "This is an effort on our part to ensure that the philosophies my daughter had about her classmates will live on. Even though her life ended tragically, we hope it will add to the fulfillment of these other students' lives. Even though we couldn't help her, we can help others."

Bryn was Susie's soulmate from the time of her birth in Dallas. Mother and daughter were constant companions, away from Denver family and friends during Mark's demanding residencies in internal medicine and gastroenterology. They returned to Denver where Mark established a following of devoted patients.

After Bryn's death, the Linkows received an outpouring of love from patients, friends and relatives. One night a huge turkey dinner for twenty with all the trimmings arrived from a patient. The Linkows called family members to come share the unexpected feast. People the Linkows didn't know well paid condolence calls, took them out for lunch and dinner, called to check on how they were doing and delivered food. "Daily I was touched by people's kindness. All these generous acts helped me get over my despondency just by knowing people care," Susie said.

Bryn's boyfriend, Devin Shaffer, was in Turkmanistan (former Russian country) in the Peace Corps when Bryn ended her life. Devastated, he returned to Denver to attend law school at the University of Denver while living with the Linkows. He adds great joy to their lives. Mark, Susie and Matt continue to give generously to others in Bryn's honor.

Contributions to the Bryn Sara Linkow Foundation may be sent c/o The Chotin Group, 6400 South Fiddlers Green Circle, Suite #1200, Englewood, Colorado 80111.

AGAPE is a Greek work meaning a selfless love that motivates people to give gifts of themselves, their time, energy and effort, serving others. The recipients can be anyone - even strangers.

Colonel William C. Ohl, Eleanor Ohl and Colonel William C. Ohl Jr.

My husband and I met Bill Ohl while living in Japan. Bill was an Army captain assigned as an R&R (rest and recreation) liaison officer while recovering from wounds received in Vietnam. A friendship quickly began which continued as we visited Bill at Army bases scattered throughout the U.S. We followed Bill's rapid promotions to colonel. One of our trips coincided with a visit from Bill's parents. His father, Bill Sr., is a retired Army Air Corps hero and Eleanor, his mother, we found as engaging as Bill. Through the years the senior Ohls have visited us and we have been to see them in Fort Myers, Florida.

To celebrate the 60th anniversary of Bill Sr. and Eleanor, the family was gathering in Fort Myers for Christmas and the December 27 anniversary celebration. Bill Jr. coordinated a touching video tracing the marriage from 1935. For three weeks, after finishing work in Leavenworth, Kansas, Bill drove an hour each way to Kansas City to work assembling newspaper clippings, the chronology of hundreds of pictures and splicing video tape.

In 1935, the country was still in the Depression following the 1929 stock market crash, the DC3 was commissioned and Monopoly hit the market. Pictures from the senior Ohl's childhood, courtship, relatives and ancestors were showcased to music from the year of their marriage.

Pat, the oldest daughter, reminisced about happy memories as photographs followed her life through childhood, teen dances, drama, musicals, marriage to Gordon thirty–three years previously and snapshots of their four children. Gordon masterfully played the harmonica as Pat sang a Christmas song.

In 1942, war headlines coincided with Jean's birth. Jean was the most emotional of the children, having to stop the video multiple times trying to compose herself so she could talk about how much fun the Ohls had as a family. Memories of her dad: Special times in Troy, N.Y. hiking in the woods behind the house, learning about integrity and developing backbone. Memories of her mother: A treasured doll, special dresses, inheriting her mother's sense of style, learning to listen, and preparing seated dinners for twenty with ease.

In 1944, the headlines reported bombers blasting Berlin, MacArthur's maneuvers and U.S. troops storming Normandy, and Bill Jr. was born. Bill is a graduate of Virginia Polytechnic Institute, an honor graduate of the Army War College, a Ranger and spent twenty–one out of his thirty years in the Army jumping out of planes. This highly trained soldier is a gentle soul. His uniform doesn't have room for any more medals. Bill's memories of his dad: Strength, security, discipline, learning to do every task well, rowing around the lake in Troy while fishing for blue-gill and bass, parasailing as a Father's Day gift, enthusiasm and pride in all Bill's accomplishments. Bill recounted taking his father in a helicopter to prepare for Bill's jump from 10,000 feet. The senior Colonel had a deathgrip on his seat. Memories of his mother: Compassion, spoiling all four children by making different breakfasts and lunches for each, being the prettiest mother and strength in crisis situations. Vietnam pictures flashed on the screen to the music of "Leaving On A Jet Plane."

1950 brought the McCarthy era, U.S. troops in Korea and Grace's arrival. Grace was a cheerleader, University of New Mexico graduate, who sensed her father's dream that she join the military but felt she was raised to think too independently to function well in the military. Grace's creative talents have flourished in her marketing and public relations career. Since the family moved so many times, Grace's best friends and support system were her family. This strong bond has continued into adulthood. The family relishes their frequent gatherings when they laugh, ski in Breckenridge and hike in Estes Park. Grace witnessed a softer side of her dad during an emotional Christmas before he left for Korea.

The video finishes with the senior Colonel Ohl parachuting at age 70 and pictures of the anniversary couple beaming with the background music of "Young At Heart."

Bill Jr. had to leave shortly after the anniversary celebration to return to work. Since all the Ohls love to dance, Bill arranged for a limousine to pick up the anniversary couple plus Pat and Jean and their husbands. Bill surprised them by having the Fred Astaire studio opened for a private dance class, with an instructor for each couple. Then they were whisked off to dinner and finally to a jazz and blues club with the expenses for the evening covered by Bill.

The video conveys not only the history of this unusual family, but the warmth, love and fun they have shared.

Families are precious things. And far

though we may roam, the tender bonds

with those we love still pull our hearts

toward home.

By Bill Mossburg

Dick Pherson was the center of my life as well as the light of it. As I remember him, I am moved to tears because of my loss of this wonderful man. Making this quilt for Dick has enabled me to feel a completion with this incredibly loving man and our life together. Dick was my partner for seven joyful years. He was born at the Presidio in San Francisco, California to Helen and Harry Pherson on November 26, 1953. He died in Denver on June 25, 1988.

Dick would want to be remembered as a friend, son, brother, and uncle and as a person who found joy in living every day of his life, and in every activity of every day. His friends and family were charmed by his laughter and happiness, whether at work with customers at Boris Kroll Fabrics or while he was cooking, gardening, dancing or traveling. He worked with Mitch and Barbara. Barbara Brown is who helped me with the quilt. Mitch and Barbara remember customers coming in, not for business, but just to have coffee and visit with Dick for a while. A local interior designer used some of their fabric in a skybox at Denver's Mile High Football Stadium. When the project was finished, Dick, Mitch and Barbara were invited to see the project and meet the owners. Barbara remembers how Dick's reaction and enthusiasm excited all of them, giving the new owners an entirely new outlook on their project. Dick had a gift of making others feel so good and so special.

Dick loved and enjoyed his family. He was a devoted son and particularly loved to be with his sister's children – Jason and Russell. Like his mother, Dick liked to chat. The two of them could stay up half the night talking with each other and anyone else who cared to join in. Home life was a real source of his joy. He loved to garden, shop for groceries (really – it relaxed him) and especially to cook and bake. He cooked as a way of loving and nurturing family and friends.

Dick and I loved to travel. Our Caribbean cruise during the mid–80's was probably our favorite and most fun trip. Dick loved to dance and participate in individual sporting activities like swimming, skiing and skating. Before and after his first bout with pneumocystis pneumonia, Dick was an avid fan of aerobic exercise. He became an instructor and won several awards in the Rocky Mountain region. Dick's energy was extreme in both directions. He was either going full steam ahead at 100 m.p.h. or sound asleep.

Everything on Dick's quilt symbolizes something about him. It portrays the Rocky Mountains of Colorado, the area in which he lived most of his life. The color red was important to us because I believed it so demonstrated his characteristics of activity, vibrancy, and friendliness. I succeeded in getting him to introduce it as a major color in his wardrobe. The two hooked rugs portrayed are of our dogs ("the kids"), Willee, the Scottish terrier and Maxwell, the West Highland terrier. Dick worked on both of the rugs while he was living his last days at the Hospice of St. John. His mother, sister, and I also helped with the hooking. The starburst in the sky represents Dick in all of his active, vibrant brightness looking down on all those who knew and loved him.

Dick Pherson was one of the most caring people I will ever know. He was always concerned about others, even strangers – like those in the grocery store who needed instruction on how to select the best produce. He enriched my life tremendously in so many ways, and still does to this day. I am grateful that I can memorialize him through this quilt and continue to love him as I proceed to live my life as fully and joyfully as he would have wanted me to.

Thank you Dick for your love.

This quilt is on display on the Mall in Washington, D.C. It has been sewn together with seven other quilts. Many quilts travel to schools around the country to create AIDS awareness.

The warmth of our friendship

flows strong and deep

leaving us memories

to treasure and keep.

You Are The Friend
I Will Cherish Forever

(author unknown)

Once in a long while, someone special walks into your life and really makes a difference.

They take the time to show you in so many little ways that you matter.

They see and hear the worst in you, the ugliest in you, but they don't walk away. In fact, they may care more about you.

Their heart breaks with yours, their tears fall with yours, their laughter is shared with yours.

Once in a long while somebody special walks into your life and then has to go their separate way.

Every time you see a certain gesture, hear a certain laugh or phrase, or return to a certain place, it reminds you of them.

You treasure the time you had with them, your eyes fill with tears, a big smile comes across your face and you thank God that someone can still touch your heart so deeply.

You remember their words, their looks, their expressions.

You remember how much of themselves they gave – not just to you but to all.

You remember the strength that amazed you, the courage that impressed you, the grace that inspired you and the love that touched you.

Lori Kneser and Sally Kneser

What I Hoped To Give

By Sally Kneser

Prior to our daughter Lori's 21st birthday, I spent a great deal of time thinking about what we could give her that would be memorable. That exercise provided an opportunity to muse about what kind of person she is, what would appeal to her, how much I love her, and what might be a lasting gift.

Since she had just completed a fabulous and expensive semester in Florence, Italy, our birthday gift had been agreed upon. We would contribute money toward her trip. But the trip had already taken place, so the thrill was just a memory. And how glamorous is it to answer your friends' question, "What did your parents give you for your 21st birthday?" with "Oh, they helped me retire some debt." No, I was seeking something non–monetary but meaningful.

I decided to modify an idea from my sister-in-law. Years ago when her daughter was one year old, she requested letters from the family that would be placed into a box. The daughter would be allowed to open the letters when she turned 21. I wrote to all relatives requesting a letter to Lori. I hoped everyone would write personally, even if it were very short, and I recommended reminiscences, predictions, advice, memories of when they turned 21, or simply best wishes.

The week prior to my daughter's birthday I gathered all the letters that had been mailed to me into an adorable cardboard box. According to reports, Lori loved the letters. She read them and cried. She read them again, and cried again.

I hope she will read them often...especially for her big birthdays when she greets a new decade. She will have the affirmation that she was loved by many. And she will have mounds of advice that no doubt seem different each time she enters a new life stage.

What I Received

By Lori Kneser

Having long passed the age when I opened numerous big and exciting presents on my birthday, I was truly surprised and excited when a large package arrived from home a few days before my birthday.

When I finally dove into the box that Saturday, I had no idea that it would be a two hour opening process. The package contained two smaller boxes. One held jewelry that my grandmother bought on her honeymoon in Mexico, and the other was filled with cards and letters of advice, love and memories from nearly all of my relatives. So much care, thoughtfulness and love had obviously been put into each card, and many of them made me cry.

I know that my mom put considerable time and planning into this gift and it is one that I will always cherish. The advice means a great deal to me now, and will no doubt take on different meanings when I read the letters again in later stages of my life. My mom knows that she gave me a gift from her heart that I loved receiving, but I am not sure if she knows just how important the letters are and will continue to be for me as messengers of comfort, love and advice from my family for the rest of my life.

Collect memories

not things.

By Midge Kuster

My gifts from the heart are the times I spend helping friends close to my heart. The first person is an 82 year old woman. I try to keep her life on an even keel. The woman is very regal and wants to remain as independent as possible. She still is able to drive, but only within the limits of San Pedro. I take her clothes shopping and to the airport whenever she goes to visit family members. Her daughter lives in Alexandria, Virginia so she is not able to assist her mother on a day to day basis. Recently my friend had a painful episode of shingles so I took her to the doctor, made sure she had meals and provided much needed moral support. She is very grateful and it is a pleasure to be of assistance.

THE GREATEST GIFT YOU CAN GIVE IS YOUR TIME. A caring inquiry means the world to someone who is no longer in a work place environment for emotional support.

I also help my bosses' family since they have no

relatives in the Los Angeles area. I baby-sit so that the parents can get a much needed R&R. They have not been used to being tied down. They were blessed with a daughter, then twins a year later. They have a busy household. In spending time with children you get much more than you give. Their pleasures are simple – a squeal of delight from a swing in the park or being read a favorite book.

One of the hardest situations to be placed in is when a loved one is dying. What do you do, what do you say?

My wonderful husband, Jim, died from cancer at the young age of 55. I never would have made it had it not been for the love and support of my children, my extended family, friends and co-workers.

Jim was a real optimist who always believed he would beat the lymphoma, but God had other plans. He didn't want people fawning over him and would become upset when I answered an inquiry as to what therapy was taking place. "Just tell them I'm ok," was his request.

But I have always been very open and needed to verbalize my suffering and fears. I come from a large family and they were my biggest support. I would come home for a hospital respite and the answering machine was full of inquiries. It was a catharsis to know that people cared in these darkest of hours. My sister, Connie, came to stay with me the two weeks before Jim died. She stepped in with a quiet grace to assist in hospital vigils and funeral arrangements.

At the funeral/wake, Jim's friends from Mary Star of Sea High School in San Pedro had arranged for all the food. Phone calls were made and the tables were bountiful. We made this a celebration of a life well lived. Afterwards friends have been such a help. A phone call to go see a movie or visit for the weekend have been my salvation.

MARRIAGE

Joy is the start of it

Sharing is the part of it

Love is the heart of it

Glory Weisberg

By Glory Weisberg

Several years ago, after my son, Steve, graduated from the University of Colorado, he asked me what I wanted for my birthday. Since I already had enough costume jewelry to open a boutique, enough perfume to stink up a neighborhood and needed no new kitchen gadgets, I asked him to make a donation to one of my favorite charities. He did, and subsequently became a member of the Kempe Auxiliary, which supports victims of sexual abuse.

Today, six years later, I still put high on my list of gift choices, which I post for Chanukah, the giving of money to favorite charities, Tzadakaha. This is a Jewish tradition referring to giving to good causes and doing good deeds.

This year when my anniversary came up, I listed "non–monetary gifts for Mom" on the refrigerator. My son sees this list often, although he now owns his own home. On that list are chores I cannot do but need to have done. My son is learning those gifts of good deeds, doing what is important to the recipient, rather than to the giver is at the heart of sharing one's important dates. An occasional bunch of flowers wouldn't hurt either, especially if they are from his own garden.

I also recall how much my relatives and I treasure homemade cards, rather than those from Hallmark. Now that we have computers, we insert cute graphics. These gifts from the hearts of my children and husband are among my most treasured possessions, those I would grab in case of a fire.

By Lois LaPhan

I grew up during the dust bowl, Great Depression, W.P.A. and all the other hardships of the 1930s. There was never much money. We lived on a farm two miles from a little town in central Illinois.

In the early months of 1930, my mother started working at a bakery in town two days a week. I was a senior in high school. Mom was saving her money for her first washing machine with a gasoline motor. We were all excited for her.

Every Saturday we went into town to get flour, sugar, coffee and other things we didn't raise on the farm. Mom and I would walk around looking in the store windows. Graduation was coming up and we wanted to get ideas to make my graduation dress. We didn't wear caps and gowns then. Nearly every girl made her graduation dress.

The dress we saw one day was such a beautiful pale blue lace that I could hardly leave that window. Every week we would go to see if the dress was still there. Mom said she could make me one like it but it wouldn't be lace. I hugged her and said, "When I get a good job, Mama, I'll buy us both a lovely blue lace dress."

The next week when we walked past the window the dress was gone and we didn't look in the window any more. Sometimes I'd hear Mom sewing. She always liked to surprise us with what she was making us so I didn't go in to see my dress.

About a week before graduation Mom said my dress was ready. I'll never forget her standing there holding that beautiful blue lace dress for me with such a loving smile on her face. She had the store put the dress away for her and each week she took in her washing machine money until the dress was paid for. With a little help from all of us, Mom got her washing machine a couple of months later. But even that didn't make her as happy as giving me the blue lace dress.

Lois was going to send me a picture of herself in her blue lace dress taken on graduation day but she died before she sent it.

HOME

is where the heart is.

Missy Sweeny

Growing up in Spokane, Washington, the best memories of my childhood are due to Missy Sweeny, mother of six, and one of my mother's closest friends. This loving, generous, jovial, caring woman was always around with a ready laugh and a willing ear. Missy's daughter, Kathy Sweeny Marzano, has been one of my sister Connie's best friends for more than fifty years. Connie lives in Spokane and Kathy is in Eugene, Oregon. They call one another frequently and take yearly trips with another childhood friend, Kay (Cullen) Richardson.

Kathy and her husband, Lou Marzano, give a great deal of thought before giving one another gifts. For their 25th anniversary Lou took their wedding certificate, inscribed in calligraphy, "Thanks for 25 wonderful years" and had it framed to present to Kathy.

For their 30th anniversary Lou surprised Kathy with a trip to the Umpqua river in Oregon. They stayed at the Steamboat Inn on the river. Lou photographed a

National Geographic-quality picture of the river, which he framed and inscribed in calligraphy, "30th anniversary memories" before having it framed. Every time Kathy passes the prominently displayed picture in their home she is reminded of their romantic trip.

Kathy gave Lou iron sculptures of cranes for their beautiful gardens since cranes symbolize serenity and love.

Lou has given Kathy Lladro pigs since they are special to the Irish. Irish legend is that a home with a pig is a happy, lucky home. This goes back to the days when the Irish built their homes above the animal's quarters. When their son Louie and his wife Jeannie bought their first home, Kathy sent them a Beleek (Irish china) pig. The young couple knew the legend so they appreciated the gesture.

When Louie was on his way to San Jose to propose to Jeannie, he stopped in Eugene to spend time with his parents and to tell his parents about the engagement. Louie had no engagement ring. He planned to give Jeannie a ring on their wedding day. His parents gave him an antique ring which Lou had given to Kathy one Christmas. It had seven sapphires representing an old English tradition, "I love you. Will you marry me?" Louie headed south with the family ring. He prepared a fabulous meal for Jeannie and proposed.

Louie and Jeannie are a couple who share jointly in

running their home. Kathy and Lou wanted to give them precious time together after the birth of their first child, Amanda Jeanne, who was born on May 10, 1996. They had all the baby things they needed so Lou and Kathy gave them a cleaning lady for six months and sent the check made out to the cleaning lady.

Kathy is very sentimental so gifts are received with great appreciation. When Kathy and Lou's first child, Louie, was born, Missy gave the new parents a rocking chair. When Louie and Jeannie welcomed their baby, Amanda, the chair was passed on to them. Now Missy's great-grandchild is rocked to sleep in this chair passed down through four generations.

Fathers Day, 1996, was Lou's first time as a grandfather. Kathy bought Lou a nearly life-size stuffed bear. The proud grandparents started photographing Amanda with the bear at two months. They plan to follow her growth alongside the bear. Lou takes the bear along in the car when he is with Amanda.

For Christmas Lou received his own toy chest filled with wrapped toys to be enjoyed by Amanda at Grandpa's house. Each toy had been carefully selected by Kathy. The Fisher Price car was so Grandpa can learn to drive with Amanda since Lou is known for his poor driving. The basketball was included since Lou loves to watch basketball.

Kathy gives a thoughtful wedding gift. She buys a silver cake cutter and server with a crystal handle and has the newlyweds' names and wedding date engraved on the serving pieces. She sends along a note wishing the couple many wonderful cakes of celebration to share together.

Missy is well loved by her children, grandchildren and extended family. She is in a nursing home in Seattle. She has Alzheimer's disease and slips in and out of being lucid. Her happy, sweet and loving disposition continues to endear her to everyone who knows her. Her hearty laugh often sings out as her children tell her they adore her.

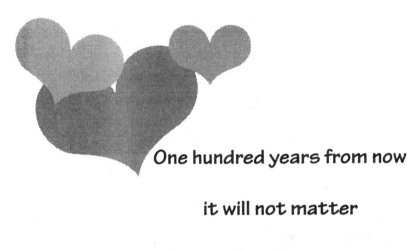

One hundred years from now

it will not matter

what my bank account was,

or the sort of car I drove.

But the world may be different

because I was important

in the life of a child.

I met a woman who said that when a friend of hers is moving out of town, she asks for cuttings from the friend's garden. The cuttings bloom and are a continuous reminder of the friendship.

Melly Kinnard

Time changes many things

but not the joy

your friendship brings.

Katie Bowlby
Age 10
Written for my grandmothers - Zara & Alberta

I recently lost my grandfather. I was very sad.

But inside I had an urgent feeling to be very mad.

I've had this loss once before.

So now I have no grandfathers anymore.

I know that they're in heaven and that they are safe.

And I will leave a spot for them in my heart

That I will call their place.

Jerry Dunn and Stephanie Dunn Blue

Laird Blue went to Jerry Dunn to ask permission to propose to his daughter, Stephanie. Jerry enthusiastically agreed. While talking, Laird jokingly asked about a dowry. At the rehearsal dinner Jerry gave a speech and said Stephanie is one of the most precious parts of his life. The dowry he gives Laird is the rich history of Stephanie's life. He brought a "dowry bag" that contained Stephanie's first Halloween costume, a bowl and spoon that she used to make scrambled egg soup and a book of love coupons. Jerry had received the coupons for Father's Day or his birthday when Stephanie was about thirteen. The coupons were for a Sunday breakfast (at home only), a massage, half–off babysitting for her younger brothers, a free win on one argument and one time when she will keep her mouth shut. The "dowry" was passed to Laird.

By Connie Emry

The best anniversary gift I gave my husband was permission to stay home and do nothing. Fred had recently taken the Myers–Briggs test, which once again confirmed that he is naturally an introvert. Though he successfully interacts in an extroverted manner all day in his professional role as an attorney, he is depleted by these efforts. He prefers the research side of his job as an estate planner. I beat him through the front door the evening of our anniversary and hurriedly lit a candle. Wine, glasses and a note adorned the table. "You may go to bed as early as you like tonight. No, we don't have to go out to dinner or to a show." Also, on the table was a box containing a sweater for him.

"The best gift you and the kids ever gave me" Fred calls the fins, snorkel and mask we gave him ten years ago, even though he has only used them a few times in tropical waters to see colorful, unusual fish and coral. He appreciated the thoughtfulness of having the mask fitted with his prescription. Without corrective lenses he could not see the underwater life forms. What a turnabout his teenage children thought it was to give their father equipment to enjoy water explorations. "Big kid" that he is, his enthusiasm usually surpasses that of any fellow snorkelers. He is closing in on sixty and this gift helps him defy barriers to the appreciation of underwater delights.

Kay, Kathy and I have been friends since grade school. Our friendship has survived different high schools, separations in college and during the busy years of marriage and motherhood. Despite moves from city to city, our closeness remains intact. I was in Europe when Kay got married and was Kathy's maid of honor the following year. Neither of them was able to come to my wedding. Since we turned forty, we have made more of an effort to get together. We talked and laughed on the Oregon coast celebrating our fortieth year. Two years in a row we met in San Francisco to continue where we left off. Challenging jobs, aging parent problems, involvements with spouses and children are things to work around. From three different cities we are currently trying to decide where we will meet next. The planning and anticipation are part of the fun. We talk of gathering in New York.

Our four children were enrolled at three Eastern universities when they coordinated a special anniversary gift for us. There must have been a lot of phoning involved. They found a remote bed and breakfast in our area for our twenty-fifth anniversary. It was very much appreciated since both of us were working full time. It was difficult for us to plan time off together. We epitomized the "sandwich generation." Between my husband's sick mother, my sick father and lots of overtime, it was a welcome respite. I particularly remember the canoe ride on the river in front of the inn, the leisurely meals and catching up on rest.

Side by side or miles apart

dear friends are always

close to the heart.

Issac and Raquel (Roybal) Martinez

When Raquel Roybal was planning her wedding to Isaac Martinez both families participated in the preparations. Three grandmothers, the mothers of the bride and groom and women from the First Spanish Assembly of God in Wheat Ridge, Colorado met for weeks before the wedding to prepare and freeze tamales, chicken mole, beans, tortillas, green chili, corn and squash for the four hundred guests. This is usual at this church. Eight ladies from the church called Raquel and said they would be honored to set up, serve, clean up and wash dishes for the wedding feast.

Isaac works full time and Raquel is a full time student and works a demanding schedule. Isaac does all the grocery shopping, laundry, meal preparation and housework to enable Raquel to study.

Nothing is impossible

to a willing heart.

Mikaela Hutchison

By Janie Hutchison

Mikaela was three years old on January 21, 1996. A week before that, her great-grandmother Jane Hutchison died. Three weeks later her great-grandfather John Shover died on February 9. Mikaela had attended Sunday School for two years so she knew about God, death and heaven. Her parents, Blake and Lora, explained to her that Jane had gone to live with God in heaven and then John followed. She seemed satisfied with what she had been told and no more questions seemed to arise.

A month later my husband Buck and I took Mikaela to a restaurant for her favorite food, spaghetti. Buck and I were dealing with our own grief daily but had decided not to talk about our parents' deaths that night and to just enjoy our special evening alone with

Mikaela. Halfway through her spaghetti, Mikaela looked at Buck and said, "Jane's in heaven." She turned to me and said, "John's in heaven too." My eyes filled with tears as I nodded. Mikaela looked first at Buck and then at me and said, "Don't worry. When John reached heaven Jane was waiting at the door. She said, 'Come on in John. Let's hokey pokey!' And do you know what guys? Jane and John are having a really good time!"

Mikaela's gift to Buck and me was to begin the process of healing our grieving hearts.

A few months later our family went to Manchester, Iowa for Jane's memorial celebration. We had fifty balloons to let go at the grave sight. Mikaela loves balloons and cried when everyone urged her to let go of her balloon since she wanted to keep it. Buck bribed her to let the balloon go by telling her he would get her another balloon after the ceremony. The following day her parents took her to Monticello, Iowa to visit John Shover's grave. She said, "John doesn't have any balloons, I'm letting this go for John." Now whenever she gets a balloon she wants to let it go for John or Jane, her great-grandparents.

Sometimes the heart sees what is invisible to the eye.

Morey and Libby Shuster   Russell and Bobbi Linscott

Bobbi Linscott was raised Jewish. Her husband Russell was raised Catholic. Since they have been married, they have celebrated all the Jewish and Christian holidays with great enthusiasm. They elaborately decorate their house at Christmas time. Bobbi has numerous Christmas sweaters. During December they send out a card with Santa and a rabbi on the front and on the inside, "Happy Whatever." Both their extended families enjoy participating in all the holidays of both religions. Shortly after meeting Bobbi, Russell participated in the laborious preparation of kreplach, delicate dough filled with cooked and shredded brisket, diced onion, eggs and seasonings. They are folded in triangles, and baked or cooked in chicken broth or boiling water. Russell saw how difficult it was for the family members to shape the delicate dough into perfect squares since they didn't have a dough cutter the correct shape. He made a razor sharp cutter out of steel, which now eased the lengthy process of preparing this family favorite.

For Christmas, Russell and Bobbi wanted to do something special for Bobbi's parents, Morey and

Libby Shuster. Most older people don't need "things." Bobbi's mother, now deceased, was blind due to complications from diabetes. Most of the time Morey and Libby ate out since meal preparation was difficult due to Morey's job. Russell and Bobbi spent an entire day preparing kreplach. They fixed meal size bags and stocked the freezer with enough kreplach for the next six months. When Russell and Bobbi presented the gift, the Shusters were so touched that they cried.

Stephanie Smookler   Allison Smookler

Stephanie and Allison Smookler are the daughters of Bobbi Linscott. Stephanie is a full-time student and works full-time so finances are tight. She was concerned about buying something special for her younger sister for Christmas. Bobbi suggested a gift from the heart. Stephanie spent countless hours going through family pictures to find pictures of the two sisters together. She didn't want anyone else in any of the pictures. She traced their lives together from the time Allison was six months old and they were dressed in matching outfits – a tap dancing recital where both girls were in tap shoes and costumes, swimming, both in cheerleading uniforms when they were in the third and fifth grades, matching bathrobes, and high school graduation. The latest picture of the two of them they had taken as a surprise for their mother. She had been telling them for months that the only thing she wanted was a picture of them.

The only thing that matters

Are matters of the heart.

Al Harris

When Al Harris returned to Denver from Vietnam, he looked up a friend he had served with in Vietnam. This friend's eight year old daughter had muscular dystrophy. She was in a body brace since she had no strength in her spine. She was strapped to a wheelchair and only had the use of her fingers. She got a cold, which progressed to pneumonia, and died in 1976.

Al was so touched by her death that he took action. He became a muscular dystrophy volunteer, helping with walkathons, spaghetti dinners and the March of Dimes telethon. He was frustrated with the high prices paid to the entertainers on the telethon and that the majority of money raised in Colorado was leaving the state for the national office. Al has ridden motorcycles since he was thirteen and raced motorcycles since he was fifteen. In 1980, he started a Colorado fundraiser when he gathered the members of his Chapter C Freewheelers motorcycle club. They met at Mile High Stadium and rode at the speed limit, not raced, in a loop through the mountains and back to Denver. Al got sponsorship through the Freedom Harley Davidson dealership. Television and radio personalities, Senator Ben Nighthorse Campbell and a child with muscular dystrophy riding in a sidecar participated. Nearly every one of the twelve years Al was involved, he raised more money than other participants in pledges by making hundreds of phone calls to friends and customers from his car repair shop, asking for donations.

Al's motorcycle club also gives money to the Anchor Center for the Blind. The club sells flowers, plants and bulbs to raise money to buy bulbs to donate to the Littleton Arboretum. When there are illnesses or deaths in the motorcycle community, flowers and gifts are bought for the struggling families.

May 6, 1992, Al's grandson, Brandon Harris, died of Sudden Infant Death Syndrome (SIDS). Not only was Al's family heartbroken, but the babysitter who was caring for Brandon at the time of his death was devastated. She is a woman who is unable to have children so chooses to care for other people's children as an outlet for her maternal instincts. Now she is afraid to care for infants and only accepts children older than three years of age.

There is no way to prevent or treat SIDS and there is no research being done in Colorado. Al knows about one team at Harvard researching genetics and tissue samples from autopsies. Since SIDS is an unexplained death, conducting an autopsy is automatic. The place of death is treated as a crime scene until a crime is ruled out. In the past, parents, grandparents and babysitters have been treated as suspects. Now that police and paramedics receive education about SIDS, there is more sensitive treatment.

In Colorado, there are a few paid staff members in the SIDS office. There is a large group of volunteers who are on twenty-four hour call, who are contacted by the police and paramedics and who are dispatched to the death scene when SIDS is suspected to support the families and caregivers. Counseling is provided at no charge. After his grandson's death, Al switched all his fundraising efforts to SIDS. He contacted Lloyd Chavez, owner of Burt Chevrolet, and asked for donated space to hold an auction. Again Al gathered his motorcycle buddies and asked them not only to donate new items but to bid high on them. Baked goods, motorcycle helmets, leather jackets, crafts, gift baskets, furniture and fishing equipment was bid on at outrageously high prices. The first year $500 was raised and now the auction brings in $10,000. To keep costs to a minimum, no pledge packets are mailed. The money raised helps subsidize the tight budget of the Colorado office and the rest is sent to the SIDS research team at Harvard. The meeting room space is no longer large enough to hold the growing auction so the service area has been taken over during the bidding.

For eight years Al has played Santa for nursing

homes, daycare centers and his own family and friends. He lets his beard grow to mid–chest and puts on his costume and boots with bells. His wife dresses as Mrs. Santa in a costume made by a friend. She dons a wig, granny glasses, a hat and carries a basket filled with candy canes. So far none of their grandchildren (the oldest is 7) have recognized them. They walk around Washington Park at Christmas time. Cars slow down, wave and honk. Their oldest son, Tim, coordinates their arrival, climbs to the roof and stomps before they appear at the door. One child who lived in a home without a fireplace asked how Santa could get in since there was no chimney. Al thought quickly and said that Santa had a magic key. Now he carries an enormous gold key as part of his costume. An older child said, "If you are Santa, what is my address?" Al said he couldn't remember the address but he could describe the child's roof. Al requested cookies from a young boy who said his house didn't have sweets since he is diabetic. Al then asked him to leave cereal for Santa and Rudolph.

Al is a friend who would be there to help if I ever needed him.

The best things in life

aren't things.

Kelly Kinnard

My daughter Kelly went to Spain as a high school student. She lived in Huelva, on the western coast with Maria, a thirty-four year old single teacher and Maria's father, Francisco. Maria and Francisco warmly welcomed Kelly into their lives. Maria is an exceptional cook who prepared a myriad of Spanish specialties, rarely preparing the same dish twice. In the summer the three moved to their second home in Punta Umbria, on the Spanish Rivera. Punta Umbria is favored by the Spaniards rather than tourists. Having an American student living there was rare. The students enthusiastically included Kelly. They marveled at her pale Irish/Scottish skin. They asked, "Doesn't the sun shine in Colorado?" They were certain that within months in the blazing Spanish sun Kelly was certain to turn as burnished bronze as they were. They had never seen sunscreen with an SPF factor of 45. Daily Kelly's new friends would come and pick her up to go around town to introduce her to everyone. They insisted she bring her sunscreen, which each person examined with giggles.

Nightlife began after eleven, which suited Kelly. The

students headed out to dance and drink until dawn. Kelly would return home at seven a.m. as Francisco was awakening. He had flamenco music blaring as he danced around the house.

There is no way I can repay Maria and Francisco for the happiness they gave Kelly. Kelly returned in August with pale burnt skin. Before going to Spain she was aware how insular Americans are. She had observed how isolated the hundreds of foreign students were at her high school. She had been involved in the Cultural Exchange Club before her trip to Spain and we had hosted exchange students. Her kindness to the students was touching. During her senior year she became president of the Cultural Exchange Club and took two Japanese girls under her wing.

The day before Kelly's junior year began, we learned our neighbors were going to host Eduardo for a year. Eduardo is from the Basque region of Spain. Before she met Eduardo she said, "I'm going to make a difference in his year here." She said we needed to go and meet him which is the Spanish tradition of welcoming every visitor. She said we weren't to shake his hand, but to kiss him on both cheeks. Kelly offered to drive Eduardo to and from school daily. From the first day of school Eduardo became part of Kelly's circle of friends. She attended a high school not known for kindness and she made certain he was not lonely like many of the other exchange students. Eduardo's English was rough at the beginning. Kelly spoke in Spanish and explained the strange American customs. Quickly the two became inseparable. Kelly would tease Eduardo about the numerous girls who had crushes on him. Paul Landauer, his American father, referred to him as the Spanish Tom Cruise.

Eduardo was taking all advanced placement classes in English. Gradually we watched as his command of English grew and he understood and used slang. For the first five months he was involved with Kelly's group of friends. In February, when soccer tryouts began, it was obvious Eduardo would be the star of the team. Through soccer, he developed friendships with his teammates who called him "Eddie." They appreciated his soccer talent and enjoyed his quick wit. We had a going away party for Eduardo and seventy-five of his new friends. His departure left a void in our lives.

Kelly continued to reach out to others when she entered Whittier College in California. Rian Windsheimer had taken over the Whittier college program helping the homeless. He asked Kelly to help him. Two nights a week she worked at the area churches that rotate hosting the homeless. During December, a synagogue hosted the homeless so the Christians could celebrate Christmas.

The best way to repay kindness

is to pass it on.

By Sharon Johnson
Jacksonville, Florida

In the fall of 1990 I had a group of academically challenged fourth grade students. We sat down together and talked about special projects they wanted to do during the school year. They came up with the idea of a garden. One of the girls' fathers donated a dozen bags of black soil and a garden hose so we could get started. I'll never forget seeing him with his hands on his hips, shaking his head and saying, "Mrs. Johnson, you're never going to grow anything in this sand." We got started by planting radishes.

Unfortunately, there were only twenty–four students in my class and county budgets couldn't support classes that small. On the eleventh day I got word that my class was going to be split and added to other fourth grade classrooms. Teachers are like mothers. We bond with our students. I did what every good mother would do if she lost her children, I cried. Never have I spent such a miserable weekend. I didn't know how I was going to explain this to my class.

I lost my class. To this day those children come back and remind me that THEY started the garden in the first eleven days of school. My principal offered me a first grade class. I told her I would prefer the firing squad. I love young children. I'm certified in Early Childhood Education and I have taught kindergarten. But I have also spent years collecting snakes, bugs and rocks that make older kids really like science. The principal's next suggestion was a combination class of gifted children from grades four and five.

Most of my teaching years have been spent in private schools. I've taught wonderful, bright and gifted children. They are so EASY to teach and they love to learn. Since I couldn't have my small group of children I had bonded with I wanted to try something more important. God bless my principal, Verna Fields. She let me try something new. We gathered twenty-four wonderful and special fourth and fifth graders. They were children who weren't achieving as well as they could. They were not learning disabled or discipline problems. Neither were they excessively motivated. They were students who didn't cause problems. They didn't raise their hands to ask for help. They were C – to D – students who were possibly at risk. I was very sure that if we concentrated on reading, writing and math we'd make dynamic progress. Boy, did we! To this day, I keep their national test scores to remind me of how hard they worked and how much they learned!

Our new group gathered and we behaved just exactly like that bright class I'd just lost. We planned, we mapped out the year and once again, the garden was in the plan.

I love those kids! They're seven years older now and they still come back. I know that the chain of events that hurt at the time was the best thing that could have happened for all of us. I have never worked so hard in all my life as I did with these kids who took over the garden, became LEADERS and EXPERTS in gardening. I led these children down rows of radishes, carrots and cabbages....teaching all the way. I think for the first time in their lives they were learning.

That first fall garden was incredibly productive. We planted everything the kids wanted to plant. Collard greens? I had never heard of them and I sure didn't know what to do with them. But my girls did. And let me tell you, we harvested them, washed them three times to get the sand off, cooked them and ate them. They were delicious. I learned so much from this class.

These kids were so brave, so in control of their gardening, that for the spring garden we decided to "adopt" younger classes – to teach them how to plant. My class was so patient. They taught younger children how to measure to plant seeds far enough apart. They taught them how to space rows. They helped them harvest what they had grown.

Our school garden is a place of harmony. We have space for all our students to plant, hoe, weed and harvest. Kindergarten hands and special education student hands work there. There is never conflict in the garden. There is accidental stepping on plants, but there is never anger or hostility. I have a little window in my portable classroom where I can observe garden behavior. I can't help looking at radishes and cabbages that get bigger overnight. There isn't any pressure in the garden either. All we have to do is remove the competition (the weeds) and let the good plants grow. A good lesson in life.

I've written several grants to gain funds to support this program in the classroom. We received the National Gardening Association Grant several years ago which provided tools, fertilizer and a compost house. We have students in the cafeteria collecting fruit and vegetables daily for the composting project. Other grants have helped us purchase a refrigerator, convection oven, hot plates, cooking pots and utensils. Seeds and soil supplies are funded by our school during a once a year fund raising effort.

Here at Lone Star Elementary we feel that our children should come to a school that is a beautiful and peaceful home away from home. Often it is more beautiful and peaceful than their own homes. The gardening project was a beginning for other projects. Flower boxes adopted and cared for by individual classes, tree planting to beautify our campus, adopting adjacent land, cleaning out trash and developing a nature walk helped us to win the Clean Campus of the Year award for Duval County.

Gifts from the heart

keep on giving.

ORDER FORMS

ORDER TODAY!
Call 800/228-0810
Fax 800/772-9165
Visit www.kendallhunt.com

Quantity discounts are available.
Call (800) 228-0810 for more information.

Qty.	Title/Author	Price	Total
	Gifts From the Heart Kinnard (ISBN 1-4423)	$12.95*	
	Get Organized! Kinnard (ISBN 1-2064)	$59.95*	
	I Need a Wife! Kinnard (ISBN 1-2541)	$19.95*	
AL, AZ, CA, CO, FL, GA, IA, IL, IN, KY, LA, MA, MD, MI, MN, NJ, NY, PA, TN, TX, & WI add sales tax.			
Add postage: $4 for the first book and $.50 each additional book			
		TOTAL	

*Prices are subject to change without notice.

❏ Check enclosed   ❏ Charge my account:
❏ VISA   ❏ Mastercard   ❏ American Express

Account # _____
Expiration Date _____
Signature _____
(Above must be completed for all charges)
Name _____
Title _____
Organization _____
Address _____
City _____
State _____ ZIP _____
Phone # (_____) _____

KENDALL/HUNT PUBLISHING COMPANY
4050 Westmark Drive   Dubuque, Iowa 52002